Celebrating
Art

Debbie and Darrel Trulson

Ad Maiorem

Dei Gloriam

• A PUBLICATION OF •

Christian Liberty Press

502 West Euclid Avenue, Arlington Heights, Illinois 60004

Table of Contents

Introduction

Art is a God-given vehicle whereby mankind can reflect the glory of the Creator by expressing some aspect of beauty, diversity or creativity. When people talk about "art", they frequently have different ideas from the next person. One may think of art in terms of a statue or a fine painting, while another may think of a child's crayon marks on the wall or their own arrangement of fresh flowers in a vase that catches the light just so. None of these images are any more deserving of artistic merit than another. Indeed, each idea of beauty and creativity is unique to the individual. Some may express their artistry through the mediums of paint or pen, while others may speak through wood or clay. The possible outlets for exhibiting our God-given talents are too numerous to detail here; yet, they are at your fingertips, available to be used as an extension of yourself.

Art is truly a creative, expressive and enriching part of our everyday lives. As you use the information contained within these pages, you must picture yourself as an observer rather than an instructor. Your child is giving you the opportunity to experience a bit of his world through his unleashing of creative skills. After initially providing the materials and location, exchange ideas together. Your main objective should be to create a time of sharing, fun and discovery rather than a "perfect" specimen of a craft.

Many young children and even some adults have had the joy of artistic endeavors forever robbed from them through the rigid, narrow-minded ideas of a teacher or other person who views themselves as holding the answers to "the right way to do things". In your teaching, it is imperative that you leave behind old baggage you may carry about art and begin anew with a fresh outlook.

It is the authors' desire that all who use this book will take time to reflect on that which is art around them. One does not need to own a Renoir or Degas to appreciate artistic beauty and presence. To make the teaching of creativity a whole life experience, one must go beyond pre-designed curricula and begin to incorporate this philosophy into their daily life.

For instance, add a centerpiece to your dinner table tonight which you or your child have created. Appreciate the beauty of handmade baskets or quilts. Savor the kitchen artistry of home-baked bread or a fragrant marinara sauce. Contemplate the differences of expression in a Rembrandt, Chagall or Michelangelo. Once all of your senses have awakened to the beauty which surrounds you, it is then you will be able to share with your child an education that far exceeds any workbook, or cut and paste session. Stretching one's mind to see past the ordinary is an important part of any person's education. Art appreciation is only the beginning. The canvas awaits; now you must pick up the brush.

Before You Begin

As you work, keep in mind that although the crafts are arranged under certain sections, they could very easily fit elsewhere. If it suits your purpose to rearrange them, then by all means do so.

We also recommend that you begin saving scraps of fabric, ribbon, broken strings of beads, etc., in a box set aside expressly for your child's artistic creations. Our intent is not to send you scurrying to every craft and art supply store looking for obscure items, but instead to encourage you and your child to be resourceful by using what is easily accessible.

You will note, that at the end of each lesson there is an intensity level rating. This star system is based on a 1-4 scale, with 1 being less difficult or time consuming, progressing to 4 which should have a greater time or material allotment. This should help you in planning your schedule and level of patience on a given day.

Section I Introduction

Using the "Gingerbread Boy" story as a kick-off to the first section, we will begin our "Crafts in the Kitchen" category. You will be the judge in this section concerning your child's aptitude with kitchen tools. Based upon their previous experience, or lack thereof, you will gauge your own level of involvement in the crafts.

You may wish to expand upon this section by purchasing some cooking magazines to look through, researching favorite family recipes, watching a cooking show or video, or touring ethnic or speciality food stores. The art of cooking is not only learned by eating various types of food, but by allowing yourself the freedom to experience food at many different levels.

Whether or not you consider yourself a "good cook" is not important. The kitchen is a place of discovery and some say the center of all that goes on in the home. Do not be afraid to experiment with your child and, if necessary, spill a little flour in an attempt to instill the love of food.

The purpose of these lessons is to provide a stepping off point for further enrichment of one's life. Some say the journey begins with one small step; but since we are gathering in the kitchen, perhaps we can begin with one small bite. Bon Appetit.

The Gingerbread Boy

There was once a good fable told about a little old man and a little old woman who lived in a little old house on the edge of a wood. They had no little boy of their own; so one day when the little old woman was baking gingerbread, she cut a cake in the shape of a little boy, and put it in the oven.

"Now," she said, "we shall have a little boy of our own, a little Gingerbread Boy."

Presently she went to the oven to see if the cake was baked. As soon as the oven door was opened, the Gingerbread Boy jumped out and began to run away as fast as he could.

"Stop! Stop!" cried the little old woman. But the Gingerbread boy ran on.

The little old woman called to her husband and they both ran after the Gingerbread Boy. But they could not catch him.

And soon the Gingerbread Boy came to two ditchdiggers who had picks in their hands. He called to them as he went by, saying:

"I've run away from the little old woman and the little old man,
And I can run away from you, I can, I can."

Then the two ditchdiggers threw down their picks, and ran after the Gingerbread Boy. But, though they ran fast, they could not catch him.

And he ran on until he came to a fat, pink pig. He called to the pig:

"I've ran away from the little old woman and the little old man,
And two ditchdiggers,
And I can run away from you, I can, I can."

But though the pig ran fast -- for a pig -- he could not catch him.

And the Gingerbread Boy ran on until he met a big, black bear. He called out to the bear:

"I've ran away from the little old woman and the little old man,
And two ditchdiggers,
And a fat, pink pig,
And I can run away from you, I can, I can."

Growling, the bear started after him, but he could not catch him. And the Gingerbread Boy ran on until he met a fox.

He called to the fox:

"*I've ran away from the little old woman and the little old man,*
And two ditchdiggers,
And a fat, pink pig,
And a big, black bear,
And I can run away from you, I can, I can."

But the fox said, "I can't quite hear you, Gingerbread Boy. Won't you please come closer and speak louder?"

Then the Gingerbread Boy stopped running. He walked toward the fox shouting:

"*I've ran away from the little old woman and the little old man,*
And two ditchdiggers,
And a fat, pink pig,
And a big, black bear,
And I can run away from you, I can, I can."

But the fox said, "I can't hear what you say, though it sounds very interesting. Step closer, please."

So the Gingerbread Boy stepped right up to the fox, leaned close to his ear and screamed out:

"*I'VE RAN AWAY FROM THE LITTLE OLD WOMAN AND THE LITTLE OLD MAN,*
AND TWO DITCHDIGGERS,
AND A FAT, PINK PIG,
AND A BIG, BLACK BEAR,
AND I CAN RUN AWAY FROM YOU, I CAN, I CAN."

Quick as a wink, the fox's jaws went "Snap! Snap!" The fox swallowed the Gingerbread Boy in two bites! Then he brushed the crumbs from his whiskers, licked his chops, and said:

"And that's the end of the Gingerbread Boy!"

The sly fox knew very well how to trick a little Gingerbread Boy who would not listen to his parents. Little children, whether real or pretend, would do well to listen to their parents and not disobey!

Lesson 1
Homemade Play Dough

PURPOSE:

In this lesson, you will be making a superior quality play dough and at the same time teaching your child the concept of taking a few raw ingredients and turning them into a useful product.

MATERIALS NEEDED:

Mix together in a medium pot:
* 1 cup white flour
* 1/4 cup salt
* 2 tbsp. cream of tartar

Combine and add:
* 1 cup water
* 2 tsp. food color
* 1 tbsp. oil

INSTRUCTIONS:

Cook mixture over medium heat, in a heavy pan, while stirring, (about five minutes). When it begins to form a ball in the middle of the pan, turn it out and knead on a floured surface till smooth. Be careful -- it's hot.

For this lesson, have your child use his play dough to make different shapes from the story. This could be but isn't limited to the man and woman, the ditchdiggers, the bear, the pig, or the fox. Allow your children to be creative and express themselves openly.

FINAL THOUGHTS:

This play dough stores well in an airtight container or ziploc bag. This recipe can be doubled easily. If you want more than one colored play dough, divide the batch before cooking and color separately. Then, cook the different batches in pans by themselves.

This is much softer than store bought play dough, and thus; good for little hands. Take out mini pans, rolling pins, cookie cutters, butter knives, etc., and let childish imaginations takeover!

This is also a great activity for hand muscle development.

INTENSITY LEVEL: * * * (Three Stars)

Lesson 2
Chocolate Pudding Finger Paints

PURPOSE:
This lesson will deal with the development of a free-form art style using chocolate pudding applied to paper. This allows the child an opportunity to have a multi-sensory experience as they see the design, feel the texture of the pudding, and taste and smell the final product created by their own fingers.

MATERIALS NEEDED:
* A few sheets of plain white paper for each child. If you want to keep the designs, use slippery shelf paper or specially made finger paint paper.
* A box of chocolate pudding

INSTRUCTIONS:
Mix the pudding as directed on the package. You may want to thin it down a little bit to make it more gushy.

Have your children smear a thin layer of pudding over the paper. Then using their fingers, spoons, or whatever else you can think of, have them print, draw or scribble designs onto their paper.

FINAL THOUGHTS:
It is recommended to dress your children in old clothes for this activity, or wear one of dad's t-shirts. The great thing about this activity is that it's okay to lick your fingers when you are finished.

INTENSITY LEVEL: * * (Two Stars)

Lesson 3
Felt Board Storytelling

PURPOSE:

This lesson utilizes the age-old method of teaching through storytelling. We will start a project here, through the making of a flannel board; which we will be using again, and adding to, throughout this series.

MATERIALS NEEDED:
* Art Pattern #7 (page 73)
* Large piece of felt, old flannel sheet, or a receiving blanket.
* Piece of plywood or corrugated cardboard to fit size of felt or flannel. Should be at least 12 inches by 18 inches.
* Colored markers, crayons or pencils
* Scissors
* Glue
* Colored squares of felt or flannel for designs (optional)

INSTRUCTIONS:

We have found that the use of felt boards are an excellent way to trace, draw and color different kinds of characters and more importantly, a good method to use in telling stories. The felt board will be used periodically throughout this series; so please keep it accessible.

The felt board can be assembled by taping or stapling a sheet of felt or flannel to the front of the 12 X 18 inch piece of plywood or cardboard. If desired, you can even thumb-tack the felt to a wall. The felt can also be designed with a background setting like trees, grass and a road.

There are basically two ways to make the figures for the felt board. The first way is: Using Art Pattern #7, have your child cut out and color each figure. Next, cut a small piece of felt and glue it to the back of each figure.

The second way is to use the Art Pattern #7 as an outline, and trace those figures on pieces of felt or flannel. Have your child cut out the felt and decorate them with markers, puff paints, sequins or other materials.

When the figures are complete, there are many creative ways to use them. You could re-read the story as your child acts out the movements of the characters; your child could re-tell the story to you using his figures; or he could create a new beginning or ending to the story. Imagine what would have happened if the Gingerbread Boy had listened to the old couple and had not run off? Have your child tell you his own version of the story. As we have said before, your only limitation is your imagination.

FINAL THOUGHTS:

Story telling is an excellent way for your child to gain a new appreciation and greater understanding of life around him. Through stories, his imagination is not merely limited to what visual images actors and directors produce for him on television. Rather, as the stories are told, the child is left to his own creativity to make up the look and feel of the characters in the story. Many people comment after seeing a movie or play, "Well, that was not as good as the book." And why is this? Simply because our own imaginations can provide so much more depth and detail than a group of actors on stage.

As your child continues to grow, encourage him to read often and share with you his adventures as he travels to far away places and meets interesting characters. He will learn many important communication skills as he relates these stories and the impressions they made upon him, back to you.

INTENSITY LEVEL: * * * (Three Stars)

Lesson 4
Macaroni Necklaces

PURPOSE:

In this lesson, your child will be designing and making a necklace of pasta. If you want to present an additional creative and educational outlet, you may consider having the child sort the pasta according to shape, size, color or simply by his own favorites.

MATERIALS NEEDED:

*   Variety of pasta with holes
*   String, yarn or other threading material
*   Paint (optional)

INSTRUCTIONS:

With the wide assortment of pasta shapes and colors available in most grocery stores, this project can have some fascinating results. It is easier to lay out the design on the table first, and then thread the pasta once your child has decided upon a pattern. Be sure to make the thread long enough to fit easily over the child's head.

If you desire a more colorful look to your necklace, you can paint the pasta by dipping/pouring water-based paint on them and then letting them dry. Our family enjoys using the tempra paints you can purchase in craft or school supply stores. If you use different colors, your child could arrange them into some interesting patterns. You may also consider using vegetable colored pasta (spinach, tomato, etc), as an alternative to paints.

This craft is not exclusive to girls by any means; boys can make some fierce looking designs with the pasta. Once again, let the child decide what they like, don't aim for perfect symmetry in shapes and sizes, just have fun and make something interesting in the process.

FINAL THOUGHTS:

Another way to broaden your scope of looking at art in all things is simply to contemplate the wide variety of shapes and sizes in the common noodle! How many different designs does your child recall from his trips to the grocery store?

INTENSITY LEVEL: * * Without Paint (Two Stars)
                        * * * With Paint (Three Stars)

Lesson 5
Elements of Shape

PURPOSE:
The five elements of shape are the basic components to all of drawing. The better we understand these shapes, the more clearly we can focus on our intended design.

MATERIALS NEEDED:
* Art Pattern #1, #2 and #3 (pages 59-64)
* Extra white paper
* Colored pencils, crayons, or markers

INSTRUCTIONS:
Review Art Pattern #1 and explain the different shapes to your children. Using Art Pattern #2, have your child draw the different elements of shape where they are missing. In addition, you may also want to have them draw the elements of shape on a blank sheet of paper. It is important to have a good understanding of the different shapes before moving on to the next Art Pattern.

When your child has a good understanding of the five elements of shape, take Art Pattern #3 and have him draw the fox in the stages illustrated. The drawing of this figure is simply a connection of the five basic shapes. Point out to your child each of the different shapes as he draws them. This exercise may also be repeated on a blank sheet of paper.

FINAL THOUGHTS:
Have your child look around the house to find the five elements of shape in the different things he sees. What elements are present in a spoon, picture, glass, car, or anything else he may come across. Discuss these shapes with your child and point out how each of the shapes are connected and related to one another.

For further information on the elements of shape, you may want to read the book, <u>Drawing with Children</u>, written by Mona Brookes. Many of the ideas from this lesson come from there.

We will be doing more work in drawing and use of the elements of shape in future lessons, so hold on to your "elements of shape" sheets for future reference.

INTENSITY LEVEL: * * (Two Stars)

Lesson 6
Edible Bread Sculpture

PURPOSE:
This lesson will be the creation of a bread masterpiece. It is entirely edible upon completion, thus giving the child the opportunity to experience raw materials turned into a useful object.

MATERIALS NEEDED FOR BASIC METHOD:
* Frozen bread dough. Prepare according to package directions. Be sure to let it rise one time before making sculpture.
* 1 egg beaten (for glaze)
* Raisins, currants, etc. (for decoration)

MATERIALS NEEDED FOR INVOLVED METHOD:
(This is if you want to make the bread from scratch.)
* 2 cups of milk
* 1/4 cup unsalted butter
* 1/4 oz. pkg. active dry yeast
* 1/4 cup warm water (105 to 115 degrees F.)
* 5 1/2 - 6 1/2 cups unbleached white flour
* 2 tbsp. sugar
* 2 tsp. salt
* 1 egg beaten (for glaze)
* Raisins, currants, etc. (for decoration)

Bread
To break it is
to share,
To make it is
to care.

INSTRUCTIONS FOR INVOLVED METHOD TO MAKE BREAD:
In a 1 quart saucepan scald milk; stir in butter until melted. Cool to lukewarm (105 to 115 degrees F.). In a large mixing bowl, dissolve yeast in warm water. Add milk mixture, 3 cups flour, sugar and salt to yeast. Beat at medium speed, scraping bowl often until smooth (1 to 2 minutes). Stir in enough remaining flour to make dough easy to handle. Turn dough onto lightly floured surface; knead until smooth and elastic (about 10 minutes). Place in buttered bowl, turn dough buttered side up. Cover, let rise in warm place until double in size (about 1 1/2 hours). Punch dough down and divide in half.

TO MAKE SCULPTURE:
At this point, either method is ready for sculpting. On a lightly floured surface, have the child sculpt his predetermined design. Keep in mind that his design may change as he works. I have seen children make chubby Teddy bears with currant eyes, snakes with knife marks down their bodies for scales, and even elaborate mermaids.

Make sure that your child makes a sculpture that is lying flat on the table. Designs which are standing up do not bake well. Use a little water to attach ears, noses, or other appendages. After your sculpture is shaped, it is ready to rise the second time. If you are using the prepackaged dough, follow the label instructions for rising and baking. If you are using the dough made from scratch, place the dough on a greased cookie sheet, cover and let rise about 1 hour. Before placing in oven, brush loaf with beaten egg to glaze. Bake in a preheated oven at 375 degrees for 25 or 30 minutes or until loaf sounds hollow when tapped. Place on cooling rack. If you used the prepackaged dough, brush the loaf with egg glaze before baking at recommended temperature.

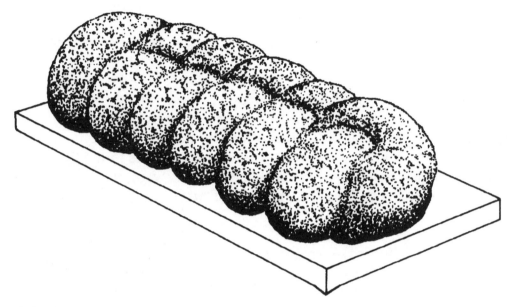

FINAL THOUGHTS:

It is a fun conclusion to allow the sculptor to eat his or her bread with lunch or dinner, perhaps even making it the centerpiece of the meal. Remember, the goal mentioned earlier: We should look at all of life as a work of art. Do not stop at the bread making itself, but continue through to the time of eating the meal. Perhaps you could create a theme meal around the design or have a special bread breaking ceremony. Whatever you choose to do, be sure to honor the artistic effort of your child and the simple joy of being hungry and being filled by an object of beauty.

INTENSITY LEVEL: * * Method #1 (Two Stars)
                        * * * * Method #2 (Four Stars)

Lesson 7
Imaginative Drawing

PURPOSE:

This lesson introduces a drawing concept which will be repeated at various times in the following lessons. Imaginative drawing is a superior alternative to coloring sheets and coloring books, because this type of drawing will encourage your student to be more creative and self-expressive.

MATERIALS NEEDED:

* Art Pattern #8 (page 75)
* Drawing tools of your choice (colored pencils, pens, markers, crayons, etc.)

INSTRUCTIONS:

Using Art Pattern #8, explain the concept to your child of using their own imagination to finish the picture. If your child is acquainted with ordinary coloring sheets, this may be difficult for him to understand right away. In this lesson we are encouraging him to be the artist and the "idea person", not to simply color someone else's picture. Please do not tell your child that his drawing is wrong or too silly, just allow the freedom of artistic expression to govern this lesson.

We are suggesting that you use this picture as a place mat for your child's dinner this evening. We have already drawn the plate, and silverware. Now have your child add the food, beverage and anything else to the picture. You should encourage your child to use the five elements of shape which were taught in an earlier lesson.

FINAL THOUGHTS:

It is important to reiterate that you should not interfere with the child's self expression in this project. You may help suggest ideas of course, particularly if he is experiencing difficulty in getting started, but let him draw and color his mat however he prefers. For example, have him visualize his favorite meal, a fantasy meal or even a silly meal consisting of a plate of worms or green eggs and ham.

INTENSITY LEVEL: * (One Star)

Lesson 8
Bean Mosaic

PURPOSE:
Lesson 8 will be the creation of a mosaic using a naturally available product. Through this craft, the child can learn effective placement of color and shape to create an aesthetically pleasing design.

MATERIALS NEEDED:
* Art Pattern #9 (page 77)
* Beans: Either a variety of natural shapes and colors (green or yellow pea, lima, pinto, etc.), or beans which you have painted different colors.
* Piece of cardboard to fit design
* Glue

INSTRUCTIONS:
Cut out Art Pattern #9 and trace onto cardboard piece. Please feel free to use your own design if you have one.

Have your child sort the various beans by colors or shapes into small cups or muffin tins. Encourage them to think, for a few moments, about what type of color groups or bean designs they would like to use within their pattern. Once they have reached a decision about their arrangement, the glue may be applied and the beans affixed to the cardboard pattern. Note: It is suggested to apply the glue directly to the cardboard, instead of each of the beans. This project must be dried thoroughly, preferably overnight, before being moved.

FINAL THOUGHTS:
It may be fun to make a pot of bean soup for dinner using the variety of leftover beans. Our favorite family recipe follows:

Any assortment of dried beans or peas you may have on hand can be used in this tasty soup.

2 cups (1 lb.) mixed dried beans or peas*
8 cups water
2 cups cooked, cubed 1/2 " ham
1 1/2 cup (3 med.) chopped onions

1 tsp. salt
1/4 tsp. pepper
28-oz. can whole tomatoes, undrained
2 tsp. chili powder
2 tbsp. lemon juice

In Dutch oven, combine beans and water. Cook over high heat until water comes to boil (15 to 20 min.). Boil 2 min.; remove from heat. Cover, let stand 1 hr. Add ham, onions, salt and pepper to beans. Cover, cook over low heat until beans are tender (about 2 hr.). Add remaining ingredients. Cover, continue cooking about 1 hour or until flavors are blended. Season to taste. **Yield: 9 (1 cup) servings.**

*Suggested dried beans or peas include: navy beans, lima beans, pinto beans, kidney beans, whole peas, split peas, black-eyed peas and yellow peas.

INTENSITY LEVEL: * * Without paint (Two Stars)
                         * * * With paint (Three Stars)

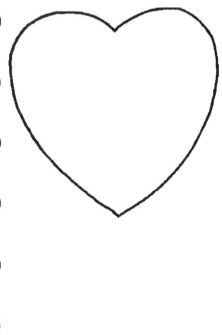

Lesson 9
Making Gingerbread

PURPOSE:

In this lesson, you will work with your child on a project which involves baking a pan of gingerbread. You may expand this lesson in any way you choose depending upon your child's previous kitchen experience. We also suggest the possibility of making a second pan for your child to give to a friend, elderly neighbor or someone of their own choosing.

MATERIALS NEEDED:

* 1 1/2 cup all purpose flour
* 1/2 cup sugar
* 1/4 cup butter, softened
* 1/2 cup water
* 1/3 cup molasses
* 1 egg
* 1 tsp. baking soda
* 1/2 tsp. cinnamon
* 1/2 tsp. ginger
* 1/4 tsp. cloves
* Sweetened whipped cream

INSTRUCTIONS:

Heat oven to 325 degrees. In small mixer bowl combine all ingredients except whipped cream. Beat at medium speed, scraping bowl often, until well mixed (1 to 2 min.). Pour into greased 9" sq. baking pan. Bake for 25 to 35 min. or until wooden pick inserted in center comes out clean. Cut into squares. Serve warm with sweetened whipped cream. **Yield: 9 servings**.

FINAL THOUGHTS:

Many times food is an overlooked form of art and creative expression in the home. With the advent of mixes and microwaves, people have lost touch with a vital part of their lives. In this lesson as well as a few others in this book, we try to encourage you to reclaim your taste buds and your celebration of the table.

Try to use quality ingredients when you cook, (i.e. real butter, pure whipping cream, etc). Just as a painter would not dream of using inferior brushes or paints, do not settle for second best when it comes to food and your family. Take your time as you prepare and then serve your family from your heart.

INTENSITY LEVEL: * * * * (Four Stars)

Section II Introduction

Throughout this section we will be creating crafts for others. Using the story of *Androcles and the Lion* as an impetus for "doing unto others", these projects will stress the concept of giving. Perhaps you can sit down with your child and think of a person or persons who would benefit from a remembrance.

In our family, the children have widowed, great-grandmothers who love receiving pictures. For this purpose, our popsicle stick frame would be ideal. Perhaps your child has a younger brother or sister who would enjoy the paper doll chain. The possibilities are as endless as the different families and situations in which they exist. The important goal here is teaching the art of giving, and encouraging your child to use their talents for the benefit of others.

Androcles and the Lion

In Rome there was once a poor slave whose name was Androcles. His master was a cruel man, and so unkind to him that at last Androcles ran away.

He hid himself in a wild wood for many days; but there was no food to be found, and he grew so weak and sick that he thought he would die. One day he crept into a cave to lie down, and soon was fast asleep.

After a while a great noise woke him up. A lion had come into the cave, and was roaring loudly. Androcles was very much afraid, for he felt sure that the beast would kill him. Soon, however, he saw that the lion was not angry, but that he limped as though his foot hurt him.

Then Androcles grew so bold that he took hold of the lion's paw to see what was the matter. The lion stood quite still, and rubbed his head against the man's shoulder. He seemed to say, "I know that you will help me."

Androcles lifted the paw from the ground, and saw that it was a long, sharp thorn which hurt the lion so much. He took the end of the thorn in his fingers; then he gave a strong, quick pull, and out it came. The lion was full of joy. He jumped about like a dog, and licked the hands and feet of his new friend.

Androcles was not at all afraid after this; and when night came, he and the lion lay down and slept side by side.

For a long time, the lion brought food to Androcles every day; and the two became such good friends, that Androcles found his new life a very happy one.

One day, some soldiers, who were passing through the wood, found Androcles in the cave. They knew who he was, and so took him back to Rome.

It was the law, at that time, that every slave who ran away from his master should be made to fight a hungry lion. So a fierce lion was shut up for a while without food, and a time was set for the fight.

When the day came, thousands of people crowded to see the cruel sport. They went to such places very much as people nowadays go to see a circus show or a football game.

The door opened, and poor Androcles was brought in. He was

almost dead with fear, for the roars of the lion could already be heard. He looked up, and saw that there was no pity in the thousands of faces around him.

Then the hungry lion rushed in. With a single bound he reached the poor slave. Expecting to meet his end, Androcles gave a great cry. But what began as a cry of fear ended as a shout of gladness. For the lion who was meant to kill him was his old friend, the lion of the cave.

The people, who had expected to see the man killed by this great beast, were filled with surprise and wonder. They saw Androcles put his arms around the lion's neck; they saw the lion lie down at his feet, and lick them lovingly; they saw the once ferocious animal rub his head against the slave's face as though he wanted to be petted. They could not understand what it all meant.

After a while they shouted to Androcles from their seats and asked him to tell them about it. So the slave stood up before them, and with his arms around the lion's neck, told how he and the beast had lived together in the cave.

"I am a man," he said, "but no other man has ever befriended me. This poor lion alone has been kind to me, and we love each other as brothers."

At first the people did not know what to do, but they soon realized that they could not kill this slave. They understood that Androcles had tamed their hearts, just as he had tamed the "King of the Jungle."

In chorus, the people rose to their feet and began to cry out, "Let the slave go!" They shouted, "Live and be free! Live and be free!", until nothing else could be heard but the noise of the crowd.

Then others began to cry, "Let the lion go free too! Give both of them their liberty!"

So Androcles was set free, and the lion was given to him for his own, and they lived together in Rome for many happy years.

Lesson 10
Popsicle Stick Frame

PURPOSE:
In this lesson, we will be creating a frame to hold a picture which your child could give to a friend or family member.

MATERIALS NEEDED:
* Popsicle sticks (at least 4)
* Glue
* Picture
* Frame decorations (optional)

INSTRUCTIONS:
The simplest method to build a frame involves gluing four popsicle sticks into a square by overlapping their ends at the corners. You may choose to leave the back open and run a bead of glue around the picture edge to attach it. Another method is to glue sticks or cardboard across the back of the frame and attach your pictures to this. Your frame will be more solid with this closed back.

After your frame is completed, you can either decorate it or leave it as is. If you do choose to decorate your frame, be sure to wait until the glue is dried. The following are a few decorative ideas which you may use for your frame:

*Use an old puzzle with missing pieces or one you do not want to keep intact and make a jigsaw frame. Simply glue the puzzle pieces on top of the popsicle sticks in an overlapping manner. We used some map puzzle pieces on our stick frame and then pasted in some vacation pictures. This gave the frame a nice "travel" effect.

*Before assembling the frame, your child could paint the sticks; perhaps choosing coordinating colors or making wild patterns of dots or stripes.

*Glue beads, fabric, alphabet noodles, dried flowers, etc., to the frame.

*Use markers or pens to write a special message around the frame.

FINAL THOUGHTS:
If you are unable to acquire popsicle sticks, a twig frame is a nice alternative. Just follow the same instructions listed above. You can also purchase stick-on magnetic strips to make your picture frame a piece of refrigerator door art!

INTENSITY LEVEL: * * * (Three Stars)

Lesson 11
Drawing Faces

PURPOSE:
In this lesson, your child will be taught how to draw facial features using the five elements of shape.

MATERIALS NEEDED:
* Art Pattern #4 (page 65)
* Crayons, markers, colored pencils or other drawing tools
* Extra white paper

INSTRUCTIONS:
Using Art pattern #4, have your child draw the development of the faces directly beneath the illustrations. Use extra white paper to make up your own faces and practice other types of expressions. Here are some examples:

MEAN   BEWILDERED   ANGRY   ASTONISHED

SLY   GOOFY   SURPRISED   HAPPY

Pay special attention as to how the eye brows and mouth can change emotional expression. (Listed above are some examples - each picture has the same face but different eye brows and mouths.)

FINAL THOUGHTS:
As your child's drawing develops, have him experiment with different expressions and faces. Using the above faces as an example, have him draw some triangle and square faces. He can try adding more detail like a moustache, freckles, eye lashes, etc.

INTENSITY LEVEL: * (One Star)

Lesson 12
Napkin Rings

PURPOSE:
This lesson will consist of creating paper napkin rings using Art pattern #10. Your child will draw the face of each person who will receive a ring at family mealtime.

MATERIALS NEEDED:
* Art Pattern #10 (page 79)
* Scissors
* Glue or paste
* Crayons, markers, colored pencils or other coloring tools

INSTRUCTIONS:
Using Art pattern #10, have your child draw a face in the blank circle of each napkin ring. You may suggest drawing each family member's face since you will be using the rings at your next meal. After the drawing and coloring, the rings may then be cut out and glued together at the "arms". Finally, the hands are to be colored, cut out and pasted on to the ends of the arm. Allow your child to set the table at the next mealtime, giving each person their designated napkin ring!

As your child draws the faces, you may want to refer him to the skills learned in the previous lesson. Allow your child to be creative, but also guide him in drawing as many details as he can think of for each of the faces.

FINAL THOUGHTS:
Due to the delicate construction of this item, it is best to use a paper napkin, as opposed to a cloth napkin, in the ring. If you need more rings, simply trace as many as you want onto construction paper and use those.

INTENSITY LEVEL: * * (Two Stars)

Lesson 13
Felt Board Storytelling

PURPOSE:
The felt board concept was introduced in Lesson 3; please refer to that lesson for additional information. In this exercise, after your child has made the felt pieces, he is to tell the story "Androcles and the Lion," to a friend or family member.

MATERIALS NEEDED:
*   Previously made felt board
*   Art Pattern #11 (page 81)
*   Various pieces of felt or flannel
*   Scissors
*   Glue
*   Crayons, markers, colored pencils or other coloring tools

INSTRUCTIONS:
Using Art Pattern #11, have your child cut out, color and decorate each figure. Next, cut a small piece of felt and glue it to the back of each figure. When the figures are completed, have your child re-tell the story of Androcles to a friend or family member using the felt board.

Another idea is to have your child invent new adventures with Androcles and his pet lion. They can be stories of what the two friends did after they left the Colosseum in Rome and started their new life together.

FINAL THOUGHTS:
After this exercise is finished, an interesting way to store your child's artwork is to hang a sheet of flannel on the wall and place the figures on it. This way, your child can play with the figures whenever he wants, and some place other than your refrigerator is decorated with the family treasures.

INTENSITY LEVEL: * * * (Three Stars)

Lesson 14
Paper Doll Chain

PURPOSE:

This is a classic American craft with timeless appeal. If your child has a younger sibling or friend, they can make an extra chain for them.

MATERIALS NEEDED:
* Art Pattern #5 (page 67)
* Scissors
* Crayons, markers, colored pencils or other coloring tools

INSTRUCTION:

Using Art Pattern #5, fold the paper into an accordion on the dotted lines and cut on the solid lines. Carefully trim around the pattern and unfold to reveal the chain. If your child wishes, he may decorate the chain with crayons or markers.

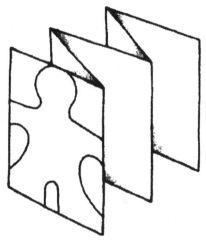

Now that your child understands the concept, he can continue making more dolls using newspaper, wrapping paper, etc. Random cutting can also be done to folded paper to create interesting geometric designs. Have your student experiment with different angles, both along the folded and unfolded edges of the paper.

FINAL THOUGHTS:

It is good to find that even in an age of wind-up, battery operated, walking, talking, burping dolls, children still enjoy the "timeless" art of paper creations. My mother would tell me how she often played with paper dolls as a little girl, and now she can watch her own grandchildren do the same. Hopefully, we will never grow so visually centered that we forget what it was like to use our imaginations.

If you are looking for decorative paper to use in crafts like this one, you can try asking local wallpaper stores for out-of-date pattern books. After visiting only one store, our family came home with six books of paper!

INTENSITY LEVEL: * * (Two Stars)

Lesson 15
Mosaic Card

PURPOSE:

Mosaic has been used as an art form for centuries. In this lesson, your child will experience making a mosaic out of construction paper. This lesson also encourages the art of correspondence.

MATERIALS NEEDED:
* Art Pattern #12 (page 83)
* Colored construction paper
* Scissors
* Glue

INSTRUCTIONS:

Cut the colored paper into 1/4 to 1/2 inch squares and separate the colors into various bowls. (Suggestion: First cut the paper into strips, then snip the squares into the bowls.) Start gluing the squares, one at a time, around the design outline in Art Pattern #12, leaving a little space around each individual piece. (Suggestion: Put a drop of glue on wax paper. Have your child then dip his finger lightly in the glue, lifting up the square of paper using his "sticky finger." Now he is ready to stick the paper square on the mosaic pattern!) Continue filling the design and snip the paper to fit the corners and curves of the picture. Finally, cut out the card and fold along the dotted line.

FINAL THOUGHTS:

If your child would like to work with real tile in a mosaic, you can try contacting a building supplier or tile store for chipped or broken tiles. Simply tell them you are doing a school project and were wondering if they would be able to donate their "discards". You can crack the tiles into small pieces, between sheets of newspaper, by lightly tapping them with a hammer. Draw the design on a square of plywood and glue the tile pieces on, leaving a little space between each one. After the tile dries, you can mix some grout and apply it into the grooves according to the package directions. The mosaic can be hung or used as a trivet.

An added idea for obtaining colored paper is to aquire the paint sample cards at hardware and paint stores. Cut these colored rectangles into small pieces and create a colorful masterpiece.

You may wish to pursue the study of mosaics even further by going to an art museum or building which contains mosaics. This art form dates back to 3000 B.C. and was originally made with round pebbles.

INTENSITY LEVEL: * * * (Three Stars)

Lesson 16
Pop-Up Cards

PURPOSE: This lesson teaches how to create a card with a 3-D effect. Your child can give this to a friend or loved one.

MATERIALS NEEDED:
* Art Pattern #13 (page 85)
* Scissors
* Glue Stick
* Construction paper (for cover)
* White paper (for inside of card)
* Colored pencils, crayons, or markers

INSTRUCTIONS:
Fold in half a piece of white paper 8 1/2 inches by 11 inches. In the middle of the folded edge, cut two slits 1/2 inch wide and one inch long. Fold the cut strip back and then fold it forward again. Open your paper and hold it like a tent. Push the strip through to the other side of your paper. Close the paper and press firmly. Open to see the pop-up strip. Draw, color and cut out a figure on Art Pattern #13 and paste it onto the strip. Finally, paste the white paper into the colored construction paper cover.

  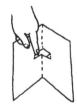 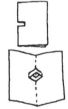 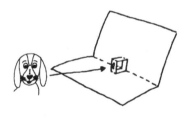

Since this is a card, you may want to draw or paste another figure on the cover and write a message. Encourage your child to think of someone to whom they can send or give the card. This could be a friend, teacher, or someone who is not feeling well.

FINAL THOUGHTS:
It is an important life skill to teach one's children to send "Thank You" notes. Making their own cards is a fun way of remembering to do this. Even with minimal writing skills, your child can express his appreciation through a hand-made card.

If you desire to learn more about pop-up cards or books, check with your local library or book store where there is a wide variety of material available.

INTENSITY LEVEL: * * * (Three Stars)

Lesson 17
Creative Bookmarks

PURPOSE:

Lesson 17 will show how to make a bookmark which can be easily tucked into a card or given to a friend.

MATERIALS NEEDED:

* Art Pattern #14 (page 87)
* Scissors
* Glue stick
* Piece of yarn or ribbon, 4-5 inches long
* Colored markers, crayons or pencils
* Glitter, stickers or other options for decorating things

INSTRUCTIONS:

Using Art Pattern #14, cut out the rectangular bookmark and punch a hole in the circle at the bottom. Color and decorate the block letters and the heart. Cut these out and glue them, in order, down the bookmark. Take your piece of yarn and put it through the hole in the bottom of the bookmark, making a knot.

FINAL THOUGHTS:

Remember that your child does not need to simply color the block letters, but they can make poke-a-dots, different line designs, or geometric shapes. If they want to get real fancy, they can use glitter and glue, stickers or whatever is around the house to make the bookmarks very special.

Bookmarks are a simple and useful gift which your child can make a quantity of and give to those who are in nursing homes or slip into a new book to give to a friend.

An assortment of blank, ready-to-decorate bookmarks can be obtained at stationary stores, J. L. Hammett or other educational supply stores.

INTENSITY LEVEL: * * (Two Stars)

Lesson 18
Personalized Wrapping Paper

PURPOSE:
This lesson will teach an inexpensive way to wrap your gifts by recycling a household item.

MATERIALS NEEDED:
* Brown paper grocery bags (Kraft bags)
* Scissors
* Colored pencils, crayons or markers
* Tempra paints or other water based paints
* Optional sponge shapes, stencils or rubber stamps

INSTRUCTIONS:
Cut the bag along the seam and discard the bottom. On the unprinted side, lay the bag out and decide how it is to be decorated. You can either stencil your design, stamp it, or even dip the child's hands or feet in the paint and press it onto the paper for a personalized effect. Put the paper aside, allowing it to dry thoroughly before using it to wrap your presents.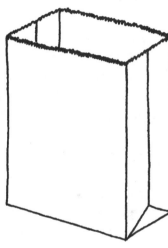

One popular method used to design wrapping paper is to take a sponge, dip an edge into the paint, and randomly sponge it onto the paper. By using different colors, it can create a dramatic effect.

FINAL THOUGHTS:
This can be an opportunity to teach your child how to actually wrap a gift. You may want to experiment first on unprinted paper to give your child practice.

A nice type of bow for this "earthy" paper is raffia, which can be purchased at any craft or variety store.

This project is also an example of how to inexpensively recycle everyday household items.

INTENSITY LEVEL: * * * (Three Stars)

Section III Introduction

Making things for oneself encourages a sense of achievement in everyone. It is this feeling of accomplishment which we want to promote in our children. In this section, your child will be creating things for himself to be played with, worn or used to decorate his own space. As we have stressed before, it is important to provide a spot for display of these and other handcrafted items. When your child senses your appreciation of their talents, they will often be spurred on in pursuit of further achievement.

Our nine year old showed a strong interest in drawing a couple of years ago and we encouraged him to pursue this interest. We initially provided him with lots of scrap paper and pencils. He then began checking stacks of drawing books out of our local library and really sharpened his skills. At this point, we bought art paper and high quality colored pencils. He is now spending so much time at drawing that we purchased a drafting table and stool for him. We use this as an illustration of how important good tools and encouragement are in the development of a skill.

Frank Schaeffer, the son of the late theologian Francis Schaeffer, recalls how even when his parents had limited resources, they made sure he had high quality art supplies. He later became a painter, filmmaker and writer. We are not saying your child will be a museum quality artist, but we are encouraging you to value artistic expression as an important part of your child's education.

The Little Engine That Could

Chug, chug, chug. Puff, puff, puff. Ding-dong, ding-dong. The little train rumbled over the tracks. She was a happy little train for she had such a jolly load to carry. Her cars were filled full of good things for boys and girls.

There were toy animals -- giraffes with long necks, Teddy bears with almost no necks at all, and even a baby elephant. Then there were dolls -- dolls with blue eyes and yellow curls, dolls with brown eyes and brown bobbed heads, and the happiest little toy clown you ever saw. And there were cars full of toy engines, airplanes, tops, jack-knives, picture puzzles, books, and every kind of thing boys or girls could want.

But that was not all. Some of the cars were filled with all sorts of good things for boys and girls to eat -- big golden oranges, red-cheeked apples, bottles of creamy milk for their breakfasts, fresh spinach for their dinners, peppermint drops and lollypops for after-meal treats.

The little train was carrying all these good things to the good little boys and girls on the other side of the mountain. She puffed along happily. Then all of a sudden she stopped with a jerk. She simply could not go another inch. She tried and she tried, but her wheels would not turn.

What were all those good little boys and girls on the other side of the mountain going to do without the jolly toys to play with and the wholesome food to eat?

"Here comes a shiny new engine," said the little clown who had jumped out of the train. "Let us ask him to help us."

So all the dolls and toys cried out together:

"Please Shiny New Engine, do carry our train over the mountain. Our engine has broken down, and the boys and girls on the other side will have no toys to play with and no wholesome food to eat unless you help us."

But the Shiny New Engine snorted: "I pull you? I am a Passenger Engine. I have just carried a fine big train over the mountain, with more cars than you ever dreamed of. My train had sleeping cars, with comfortable berths; a dining-car where waiters bring whatever hungry people want to eat; and parlor cars in which people sit in soft arm-chairs and look out of big plate-glass windows. I carry the likes of you? Indeed not!" And off he steamed to the roundhouse, where engines live when they are not busy.

How sad the little train and all the dolls and toys felt!

Then the little clown called out, "The Passenger Engine is not the only one in the world. Here is another coming, a fine big strong one. Let us ask him to help us."

The little toy clown waved his flag and the big strong engine came to a stop.

"Please, oh, please, Big Engine," cried all the dolls and toys together. "Do pull our train over the mountain. Our engine has broken down, and the good little boys and girls on the other side will have no toys to play with and no wholesome food to eat unless you help us."

But the Big Strong Engine bellowed: "I am a Freight Engine. I have just pulled a big train loaded with costly machines over the mountain. These machines print books and newspapers for grownups to read. I am a very important engine indeed. I will not carry the likes of you!" And the Freight Engine puffed off indignantly to the round-house.

The little train and all the dolls and toys were very sad.

"Cheer up," cried the little toy clown. "The Freight Engine is not the only one in the world. Here comes another. He looks very old and tired, but our train is little, perhaps he can help us."

So the little toy clown waved his flag and the dingy, rusty old engine stopped.

"Please, Kind Engine," cried all the dolls and toys together. "Do pull our train over the mountain. Our engine has broken down, and the boys and girls on the other side will have no toys to play with and no wholesome food to eat unless you help us."

But the rusty old engine sighed: "I am so tired. I must rest my weary wheels. I cannot pull even so little a train as yours over the mountain. I can not. I can not. I can not."

Then indeed the little train was very, very sad, and the dolls and toys were ready to cry.

But the little clown called out, "Here is another engine coming, a little blue engine, a very little one, but perhaps he will help us."

The very little engine came chug, chugging merrily along. "What is the matter, my friends?" he asked kindly.

Oh, Little Blue Engine," cried the dolls and toys. "Will you pull us over the mountain? Our engine has broken down and the good boys and girls on the other side will have no toys to play with and no wholesome food to eat, unless you help us. Please, please, help us, Little Blue Engine."

"I'm not very big," said the Little Blue Engine. "They use me only for switching in the yard. I have never been over the mountain."

"But we must get over the mountain before the children awake." said all the dolls and the toys.

The very little engine looked up and saw the tears in the doll's eyes. And he thought of the good little boys and girls on the other side of the mountain who would have no toys and no wholesome food unless he helped.

Then he said, "I think I can. I think I can. I think I can." And he hitched himself to the little train.

He tugged and pulled and pulled and tugged and slowly, slowly, slowly they started off.

The toy clown jumped aboard and all the dolls and the toy animals began to smile and cheer.

Puff, puff, chug, chug, went the Little Blue Engine. "I think I can -- I think I can -- I think I can -- I think I can -- I think I can -- I think I can -- I think I can -- I think I can -- I think I can."

Up, up, up. Faster and faster and faster and faster the little engine climbed until at last they reached to top of the mountain.

Down in the valley lay the city.

"Hurrah, hurrah," cried the happy little clown and all the dolls and toys. "The good little boys and girls in the city will be happy because you helped us, kind Little Blue Engine."

And the Little Blue Engine smiled and seemed to say as he puffed steadily down the mountain. "I thought I could -- I thought I could -- I thought I could -- I thought I could -- I thought I could -- I thought I could -- I thought I could -- I thought I could -- I thought I could."

The Lion and the Mouse

One evening long, long ago a lion was asleep in the forest. A party of mice, who lived in the forest, saw the King of the Beasts sleeping.

"What a huge animal he is!" exclaimed the youngest mouse, whose name was Fuzzytail.

"Yes," said his brother, Grayskin. "And it is only because he is asleep that we dare to be near him."

"Even when he is asleep, I am afraid of him," said another mouse. "Suppose he should wake up!"

"No danger," said Fuzzytail. "He is sound asleep and will sleep until the sun rises."

"I wouldn't be too sure," said Grayskin. "It is said that all cats sleep with one eye open."

"Well, you see this big cat has both of his shut," argued Fuzzytail. "I am going to jump on him."

"Be careful how you run over him. So long as you play on his back and sides, his fur will keep him from feeling your feet; but keep away from his nose, it is very sensitive," warned Grayskin.

"Eek -- Eek!" laughed Fuzzytail. "Watch me run right over his nose."

With a sudden movement the King of the Beasts opened his eyes and shook his head. All the mice scampered away as fast as they could. But poor little Fuzzytail was right on his nose, and before he could escape, the Lion stretched out one great paw and caught him.

"Gr-rr-rr!" growled the Lion.

"Oh, great King of the Beasts," begged the trembling little mouse, "please let me go."

"Gr-rr-rr!" the Lion growled again. "Why should I? Haven't you been told that it is dangerous to rouse a sleeping lion? With my paw I can crush you, you silly little animal."

"Oh, please don't," begged Fuzzytail again. "I didn't mean to wake you, and I'll never do it again."

"Well," said the Lion, "I see that you are very young, so I will spare you this time." And lifting his huge paw, he allowed the trembling

little mouse to run into the forest.

After that Fuzzytail and his friends played far away from the sleeping Lion. But one evening, as they came out of the forest, he was not asleep as usual. He was rolling around and roaring so that the whole forest echoed.

"What is he roaring at?" they asked one another.

"I am going to see," said Fuzzytail. The others begged him not to go, but the little mouse was determined.

"He set me free when he could have crushed me," he said. "Now he is in trouble and I am going to help him if I can."

As he came close, he saw the King of the Beasts, tangled up in the meshes of a net that hunters had spread for him. The more he roared and rolled about, the more entangled he became.

Suddenly he heard a little voice close to his ear. He stopped his roaring and listened. The voice came again.

"I am the mouse your freed," it said. "If you will just lie still, I will gnaw the ropes that hold you."

The huge Lion lay still and Fuzzytail gnawed at one rope after another with his sharp little teeth. At length the meshes of the net fell away, and the Lion sprang to his feet.

"Thank you, little brother," he said. "I did not know that my deed of kindness would bring me such a rich reward."

And from that day onward, the Lion and the little mouse were best of friends.

Lesson 19
Paper Plate Masks

PURPOSE:

In lesson 19, your child will create a mask made from a paper plate which he can use in imaginative play.

MATERIALS NEEDED:
* Paper plate
* Scissors
* Glue stick
* Popsicle stick
* Colored markers, crayons or pencils
* Optional decorative items (glitter, curly ribbon, feathers, lace, yarn, tin foil, etc.)

INSTRUCTIONS:

Cut your paper plate in half, and draw two circles in the plate where the eyes will go. Cut out the eyes and draw eye brows, (refer back to Lesson 11 for ideas on expression.) Cut out a piece of scrap colored construction paper, fold it into a triangle and glue it onto the face of the mask to act as a nose. Finally, glue the popsicle stick to the bottom of the mask, off to one side, for your child's use in holding the mask to his face. You could also punch holes in the sides of the mask and loop string through the holes, so the child could tie the mask to his face.

When it comes to decorating the mask, you have a number of possibilities. Coloring the mask is the most basic, but if you want to add some flair, have your child glue on strips of curly ribbon for the hair, glitter for the cheeks, crepe paper for a beard, etc. Feathers, tin foil or anything you have around the house can be added for decorations on the mask.

FINAL THOUGHTS:

For those "nothing to do days", it is a help to have a box of make-believe and dress-up clothes handy. This can include some of dad's old shirts and ties, mom's shoes and beads, and any other assortment of cast-off clothing. After mask making, your child could dress up and don their mask to become whatever their imagination desires.

INTENSITY LEVEL: * * * (Three Stars)

Lesson 20
Lunch Bag Puppets

PURPOSE:
In this lesson, your child will be making puppets, from plain lunch bags, to be used in imaginary play.

MATERIALS NEEDED:
* Art Pattern #15 (page 89)
* Paper lunch bag
* Scissors
* Glue stick
* Yarn scraps
* Colored markers, crayons or pencils
* Ribbon for bow (optional)

INSTRUCTIONS:
This puppet will be assembled on the wide side of the bag. The fold of the bag will be the clown's mouth.

Begin by cutting out the Art Pattern #15 pieces and coloring them in "clown" colors. Demonstrate to your child how the puppets mouth functions, (by placing your hand inside the bag and moving the mouth), so he can understand where the pieces are to be glued. On the pattern, the bottom mouth goes on the bag beneath the flap and the top mouth is attached to the flap. After gluing the mouth and face pieces onto the bag, your child can glue the yarn hair onto the clowns head. If you have a wide piece of ribbon, you can glue it at the neck of the puppet. Now all that is left for your child to do is come up with a circus act. Happy clowning!!!

FINAL THOUGHTS:
If you happen to have a pom-pom ball, you could use that for your clown's nose. A leftover birthday hat could be cut into a flat piece and glued onto the top of the bag to make a clown hat.

If you are in need of an area to display your child's artwork as it accumulates, perhaps you can make a "craft clothes line". Simply put two small nails or tacks in the wall at opposite points from each other (6-8 feet apart). If you do not have a wall that narrow, you could stretch the line diagonally across the corner of a room. Run a line of twine or jute string, knotting the ends onto the nails, and you're all ready to display. Use spring-style clothespins to hold up the artwork, and your child can arrange and decorate as much as he wants.

INTENSITY LEVEL: * * * (Three Stars)

Lesson 21
Juice Lid Sun Catchers

PURPOSE:

In lesson 21, you will be making a window decoration, (in the style of the old-fashioned tin punch), and have fun pounding and banging to create the design.

MATERIALS NEEDED:
* Art Pattern #16 (page 91)
* Tin lid from a frozen juice concentrate can
* Block of wood approximately 8 inches square
* Scrap piece of wood suitable for pounding
* 1 1/2 - 2 inch nail
* String
* Tape

INSTRUCTIONS:

Place the 8 inch block of wood on a solid surface and use the base for pounding your design. (Hint: If necessary, you may lay a folded towel under the wood to lessen the noise and impact.) Lay the juice lid on top of the wood and tape the design of choice from Art Pattern #16 onto it. You may also want to tape the lid to the wood to secure it from moving during the process. After a couple of practice hits on the nail, using the smaller piece of wood as a hammer, have your child pound the nail into each dot to create their design. The nail should only be pounded about 1/8 of an inch, or until the point of the nail punctures the lid. Upon completion, simply remove the tape and paper design, thread the string through the top hole, and hang the sun catcher in a bright window.

FINAL THOUGHTS:

These sun catchers also make great Christmas tree ornaments to keep or give away.

Windows are a favorite hanging place in our family. One child uses a favorite window as the place to hang paper snowflakes in the winter, leaves in the fall, and hearts around Valentine's day. The older boys have mobile sun catchers, and there is a collection of antique cookie cutters on the kitchen window ledge.

There seems to be something about the idea of a window that attracts people. We even refer to our eyes as the "windows of our souls." If you do not have available windows or you prefer other nooks and crannies for your collections, then by all means utilize those spaces.

INTENSITY LEVEL: * * * * (Four Stars)

Lesson 22
Collage Expressions

PURPOSE:

With this craft, your child will have an opportunity to express his interests, desires and ambitions by creating a two-dimensional collection of ideas.

MATERIALS NEEDED:
* Poster board, cardboard or sheet of paper
* Scissors
* Glue or glue stick
* Personal choice of magazines, photographs, drawings, postcards, newspapers, fabric, cutout letters, maps, etc.

INSTRUCTIONS:

Your child's first step is to find an idea or theme for his collage. After assembling the chosen materials, he can begin arranging them on the paper or board until a pleasing design has been achieved. At this point, he may glue the pieces in place. When it has dried, you are ready to display.

FINAL THOUGHTS:

In our family, we have created refrigerator collages using cooking magazines. We cut out pictures of our favorite foods and then arrange them in a pleasing design. The children have also created goal oriented collages using pictures to portray their interests and ambitions for the future. One of our favorite collages is an art postcard assembly using postcards gathered at art galleries and museums. We arrange them in an acrylic box frame (available at any craft supply store), creating an eclectic montage of modern, impressionist and renaissance art. Our second son made a comic strip collage simply using the daily newspaper "funnies" section. As you can see, the ideas are limitless, so the directions must allow time for the child to settle on his own form and design.

Extra collage items, in case you are stumped:
* <u>Vacation collage</u>: postcards, tollbooth tickets, restaurant menus, etc.
* <u>Business card collage</u>: Dad and Mom can help out with this collection.
* <u>Photograph collage of an event</u>: As we write this in the cafe of our favorite bookstore, we are looking at a collage of photographs taken at book signings and other store events. You can have fun cutting around the shapes of people and buildings.
* <u>Button collage</u>: An adult's help with a hot glue gun would be useful here, or the buttons could even be sewed onto fabric.

INTENSITY LEVEL: * * (Two Stars)

Lesson 23
Cinnamon Ornament Dough

PURPOSE:
Your child will enjoy an active role in holiday decorating by creating beautiful scented ornaments from this dough.

MATERIALS NEEDED:
* 4 cups flour
* 1 cup salt
* 1/4 cup cinnamon
* 3 tablespoons nutmeg
* 2 tablespoons ground cloves
* 1 1/2 cups lukewarm water
* 1 egg white

* Cookie cutters
* Rolling pin
* Yarn or ribbon for hanging

INSTRUCTIONS:
Sift the first five dry ingredients together. Add water to create a dough of modeling clay consistency. Preheat oven to 300 degrees. Roll dough out to at least 1/2 inch thickness and cut out, using cookies cutters or a paper pattern of your own. Transfer designs to an ungreased cookie sheet and using a toothpick or pencil, poke a hole into the dough for hanging.

Bake the ornaments for about one hour. Allow to harden on the cookie sheets for about ten minutes before removing to wire cooling racks. When the ornaments are completely cool, string yarn through the holes and hang from the Christmas tree or windows.

FINAL THOUGHTS:
For an added bit of Christmas fun, you can purchase a small (3-4 foot high) potted pine tree for use as a "kitchen tree". Cover the pot with burlap and tie with jute string for an added decorative touch. Decorate the tree with this lesson's ornaments, gingerbread people, popcorn or cranberry strings, antique cookie cutters or lightweight kitchen tools, and top with a ribbon tied into a bow with ends trailing down the tree. After the holidays, your kitchen tree can be planted in the yard for year round enjoyment.

Using varnish on these ornaments increases their life span. Once, our family created necklaces for the children's Grandmothers, using a heart shaped design and stringing it on a thin satin ribbon.

INTENSITY LEVEL: * * * * (Four Stars)

Lesson 24
Origami Hat

PURPOSE:
This lesson will introduce your child to the ancient art of paper-folding, beginning with a sample hat. Ideas for creating "party" hats will also be included.

MATERIALS NEEDED:
* Double-page newspaper sheet or similar size paper.

INSTRUCTIONS:
Fold the paper according to the diagrams below. There are two hat designs illustrated. The first one is easier to make then the second.

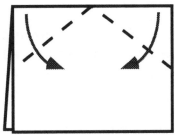

Step 1

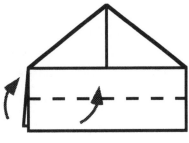

Step 2

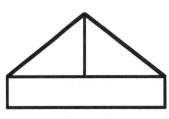

Step 3

Second hat design:

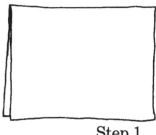

Step 1

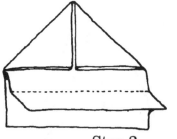

Step 2

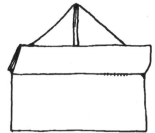

Step 3

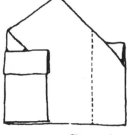

Step 4

Step 5

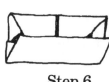

Step 6

Step 7

FINAL THOUGHTS:
To create party hats (either alone or as a group party project), use an 18 x 9 inch piece of poster board and trace the shape shown here. Cut out, roll into a cone, and glue into place along the leading edge.

Your child can use crayons, markers, glitter or stickers to decorate the hat. Curly ribbon can also be used as streamers falling from the top of the hat. Simply gather a bunch of the ribbon, feed it through the top of the cone, and tie with a knot inside. To hold the hat upon the child's head, glue a piece of ribbon or string on each side inside the cone to use as a tie (a glue gun works well here). Then let the party begin!!!

Hats are fun for make-believe play. Origami hats can be decorated to represent a policeman, nurse, chef, etc. Our six-year-old likes to make smaller sized hats for his stuffed animals to wear to their pretend parties.

INTENSITY LEVEL: * * (Two Stars)

Lesson 25
Imaginative Drawing

PURPOSE:
As in earlier lessons of this type, your child will be the "idea person" in a drawing project.

MATERIALS NEEDED:
* Art Pattern #17 (page 93)
* Crayons, markers, colored pencils or other coloring tools
* Scissors

INSTRUCTIONS:
Since your child is by now familiar with this concept of drawing, you should not need much introduction or explanation. After briefly refreshing his memory (see Lesson 7 for examples), let him get busy. The idea here is for your child to create a t-shirt design which he would like to wear. Cut out the t-shirt in Art Pattern #17 and have your child decorate it anyway he likes. This could include, but is not limited to: a school or team logo, a favorite book or movie, a message of his choice, etc. You can turn the design over if he would like to make a back to the shirt.

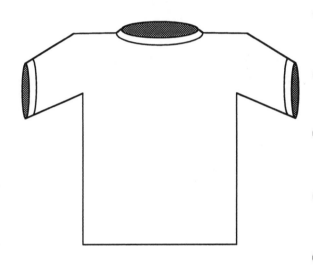

FINAL THOUGHTS:
If you and your child would like to take this idea one step further, you could purchase fabric crayons or paints, and transfer the design onto a plain t-shirt. This is a fun party project also. Instead of "goody" bags, each person creates their own wearable art.

INTENSITY LEVEL: * (One Star)

Lesson 26
Tic-Tac-Toe Felt Game

PURPOSE:
In this lesson, your child will use the felt board to learn and play a game of tic-tac-toe.

MATERIALS NEEDED:
* Art Pattern #18 (page 95)
* Felt board
* Felt pieces
* Scissors
* Glue
* Crayons, markers, colored pencils or other coloring tools

INSTRUCTIONS:
Using Art Pattern #18, cut out each of the game pieces. Each piece can be colored or designed according to your child's choosing. After coloring, a scrap of felt about 1 and 1/2 inches square should be glued to the back of each game piece.

The game board can be designed by either using felt or paper strips. Simply cut four pieces of felt eight inches long and one inch wide. These can be laid in a "#" pattern on the felt board. If you are using paper strips, repeat the process and glue felt scraps to the back of each piece of paper.

FINAL THOUGHTS:
If your child is interested, he can adapt other games to the felt board, such as checkers or even a memory game.

By now, you have probably accumulated quite a few felt pieces. A good way to keep them separate is to put them in quart size zip-top bags and label them with a waterproof marker.

INTENSITY LEVEL: * * (Two Stars)

XOXOXOXOXOXO

Lesson 27
Faded Picture

PURPOSE:
This lesson will show your child how to create an abstract design, using household odds and ends and the sun's rays. (Note: Begin this project early on a sunshiny day.)

MATERIALS NEEDED:
* Black construction paper
* Buttons, paper clips, leaves, black paper shapes, etc.
* Rubber cement
* Sunlight (should be a very sunny day)

INSTRUCTIONS:
Be sure the black construction paper is new so the color hasn't faded. Lay the paper in a sunny spot and have your child arrange his items in a design of his choosing. If he uses leaves or paper shapes, apply a bit of rubber cement to the underside to secure them. The glue can be rubbed off later. By the end of the day, the objects can be removed and the paper will be appropriately faded everywhere except where the objects were laid.

FINAL THOUGHTS:
This also can be a fun way to design cards. Just fold the paper in half, create the design, then glue writing paper to the inside. Grandma will be amazed!!!

INTENSITY LEVEL: * (One Star)

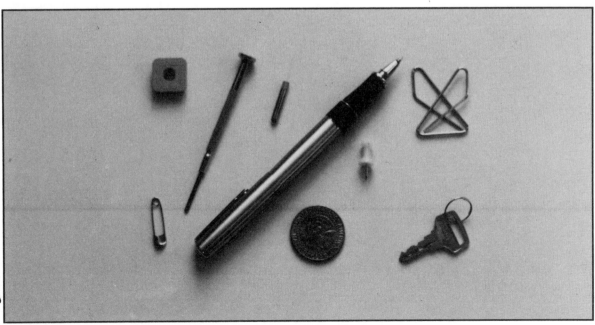

Section IV Introduction

You and your child will enjoy the art of nature in this section. Some of the crafts will involve the use of naturally available materials; others will be things which you can make for use outdoors; and finally, we will have some "just for fun" crafts that imitate things found in nature.

There are so many ways to enjoy the outdoors and changing seasons. Sometimes, when our family cannot get outside to play and explore, because of inclement weather, we bring the outdoors, inside to us. On one such occasion, we filled a large granite-ware tub with fresh snow and placed it over a tarp on the kitchen table. The mitten-wearing children, then proceeded to build mini-snowmen and make snowballs. Everyone had fun, and the family was given the opportunity to experience an interesting aspect of nature.

The way you choose to experience the out-of-doors is entirely up to you. We recommend though, that you involve as many members of your family as possible. As the old saying goes, "The more -- the merrier."

The Hare and the Tortoise

ne day there were many animals playing together. The hare liked to brag and thought he was better than all the other animals.

The hare hopped over to the tortoise. He said, "You are very slow and pokey."

All the animals watched the hare and the tortoise. They wondered what the tortoise would say.

The tortoise lifted his head high in the air. He said, "Mr. Hare, I would like to have a race with you."

The hare laughed and laughed. "Your short legs are too slow to race against me."

When the hare stopped laughing, he agreed to race the tortoise. The fox told them the rules of the race.

All the animals decided where the race should take place. They found a big tree by a stream to use for the finish line. The fox told the hare and the tortoise to line up at the starting line. The fox barked, "GO!"

The hare ran so fast down the course that the animals could not see him. The tortoise was very quiet. He kept walking and walking. He was not going fast, but he was steady and sure.

"I do not have to hurry," said the hare. "The tortoise is slow. He cannot win the race." The hare looked back and did not see the tortoise. "He will never catch up to me," said the hare. "I will sit down and take a nap."

The tortoise kept walking on and on. He did not stop. Finally, the tortoise passed the hare sleeping by the path. The tortoise chuckled to himself and kept on walking.

When the hare awoke he stretched and yawned. "I will now win the race," he said. Looking up to the finish line, the hare saw that the tortoise was close to the goal. "I must run fast to catch him."

The hare ran as fast as he could. He passed trees, bushes, and big rocks. No tortoise. Where was the tortoise, he thought?

The tortoise saw the finish line ahead of him. "I am slow," he said, "but I keep on trying."

At last the hare saw the tortoise nearing the finish line. "Oh no," said the hare, " the tortoise will win the race."

The hare could not pass the tortoise. The tortoise crossed the finish line and won the race. All the animals cheered and cheered. The tortoise was happy. The animals said, "He might be slow, but he kept on going. He did not give up!"

Lesson 28
Bird Feeders: Pine Cone or Pretzel

PURPOSE:
In this lesson, you and your child may choose to build two types of bird feeders. Both are easy to create and fun to observe.

MATERIALS NEEDED:
* Large pine cones or large Dutch-style pretzels (how many you use is up to you)
* Peanut butter (inexpensive brand)
* Birdseed
* Cookie sheet
* Yarn or string
* Butter knife
* Newspaper or wax paper

INSTRUCTIONS:
Spread your birdseed on a cookie sheet and set aside. Lay a piece of newspaper or waxed paper across the table and have your child start coating the pine cones or pretzels with peanut butter. (This part is messy, but it can also be a lot of fun for the child to smear and rub peanut butter without being told "no" -- like making mud pies.) After the entire surface is covered, roll the pine cone in the birdseed or if you are using pretzels, press each side into the seeds. When you have finished coating with birdseed, simply cut string or yarn long enough to secure your feeder from a tree or bush limb. Now all you need is a bird watcher's guide because before long, birds will be flocking to your feeder.

FINAL THOUGHTS:
We recommend fall or winter for this activity, due to the perishability of the peanut butter in the hot summer sun.

If you have a suitable tree or bush in your yard, it is fun to make it into a bird tree. Use your pine cone or pretzel feeders, strings of popcorn or cranberries (we use the strings leftover from our Christmas tree), scraps of stale bread or crackers, etc. You local library has many ideas for outdoor bird feeding.

If you and your child do not have a yard, perhaps you could hang your bird feeder from an overhang above a window or balcony. You may also be able to contact a park or forest preserve to see if they can use your feeder.

INTENSITY LEVEL: * * (Two Stars)

Lesson 29
Cardboard Racing Tortoise

PURPOSE:
This lesson will enable your child to first create and then play with their own game.

MATERIALS NEEDED:
* Art Pattern #19 (page 97)
* Shirt Cardboard or other lightweight cardboard
* Scissors
* Pencil
* Colored markers, crayons or pencils
* Ten feet of string (kite string or packaging string)

INSTRUCTIONS:
Cut out the tortoise design from Art Pattern #19, lay the design on the cardboard and trace around it. Have the child decorate the turtle with fun patterns and colors. Cut out the cardboard turtle (little hands may need help here), make a string hole and thread the string through. Tie one end of the string to a sturdy chair or table leg, have the child hold the other end of the string with the turtle nearest him. The feet of the turtle should be touching the floor. As the child pulls the string taut and then quickly releases it, the tortoise will begin flopping towards the finish line. Make two tortoises and have a race with your child. It is more interesting when a parent or sibling joins in the fun.

INTENSITY LEVEL: * * (Two Stars)

Lesson 30
Nature Mobile

PURPOSE:
Your child will have the opportunity, in this lesson, to use their collection of outdoor finds in the making of a mobile.

MATERIALS NEEDED:
* Twigs of varying lengths
* String (preferably cotton twine)
* Nature finds (shells, acorns, small pine cones, etc.)
* Choose whatever is easily available to you from this list:
   --A hand-held drill (either electric or manual)
   --A hot glue gun
   --Carpenter's glue

INSTRUCTIONS:
Gather the collection together and determine the weight of the individual items. This is a good opportunity for your child to see, firsthand, how equal weights balance. Choose the first two or three items to be hung at either end of the largest twig. If you choose to hang three items, the third can go right in the middle of the twig. Be sure to experiment with the balance before permanently attaching something to the twig; otherwise, you may end up with a lop-sided mobile.

If, for example, you have chosen shells, you will need to use the hand drill to carefully puncture a hole at the top of the shell for the string to go through. Another possibility, which will not allow as much freedom of movement but will still work, is the hot glue gun or carpenter's glue. With either of these methods, you would glue the object directly to the string.

Continue, on adding tiers to the mobile as you and your child find visually appealing objects to use. You can hang the strings from the bottoms of the first items and tie a twig and more objects from there. Or, simply skip the twigs and attach the items from string to string.

Once you have completed the project, you can suspend it from the ceiling as a gently twirling reminder of the times spent collecting outdoors.

<u>**FINAL THOUGHTS**</u>:
If for some reason your child is unable to make a collection of the type we just suggested, than by all means change it to suit their needs. Perhaps someone you know could give your child objects from nature which they have found interesting. Maybe you have a relative who lives near a beach or forest, and they could mail items to your child in order to acquaint them with another geographical area. You could also change the entire concept and create a mobile using other objects. Our nine-year-old son loves making origami and he is quite good at it. Using origami pheasants, mice, swans and stars, he made a mobile for his room. Instead of twigs, he used chopsticks to suspend his paper foldings. Use your imagination and whatever is available to you in order to create an individualized product.

Another good idea would be to use baseball cards and suspend them from miniature bats.

<u>**INTENSITY LEVEL**</u>: * * * * (Four Stars)

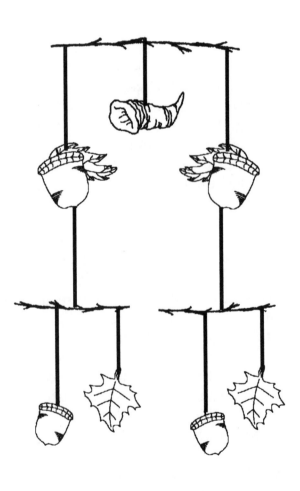

Lesson 31
Tissue Fish

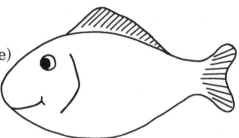

PURPOSE:

In this lesson, your child will make delicate, "just for fun" fish to hang as a mobile or as a single decoration.

MATERIALS NEEDED:

* Art Pattern #20 (page 99)
* Tissue paper (any colors)
* Elmer's glue (glue sticks do not work well here)
* Marker or pen for drawing features
* Scissors
* Tissue paper scraps or toilet paper
* Sewing thread or fishing line for hanging

INSTRUCTIONS:

Cut out Art Pattern #20 and carefully trace the design onto a double piece of tissue paper. It may work best if your child cuts out the design while you help hold the two sheets of tissue paper together. (This is delicate paper to work with, but it is very pretty in this particular project.) After the design has been cut, take one piece of paper and have your child run a thin bead of glue around the outline, making sure to keep the tail open. You may wish to draw a fine pencil line around the outline to guide the glue application. Carefully place the second fish cutout on top of the glue, matching it evenly to the bottom cutout. Let this dry for a short while, then have your child use his marker to draw the face and gills.

Using toilet paper or left over scraps of tissue paper, gently stuff the fish with a pencil to carefully push the paper forward. After filling, glue the tail closed and let dry. When you're ready to hang the fish, thread a needle, knotting the end several times, and poke it through the top of the fish. These fish are so light that you can just tape the thread to the ceiling or wherever you choose to hang them.

FINAL THOUGHTS:

Our six-year-old has three of these fish hanging above his bunk bed and he blows on them to make them "swim". You can tie these in varying lengths from a stick to look like a fishing rod with a great catch!

Your child may wish to make several fish and turn his room into a hanging aquarium! Go ahead and experiment with different designs and teach your child the names and habits of these different fish.

INTENSITY LEVEL: * * * (Three Stars)

Lesson 32
Wax Paper Leaves

PURPOSE:
In this lesson, you and your child will have the opportunity to gather colorful fall leaves and preserve them for long-lasting enjoyment.

MATERIALS NEEDED:
* Leaves in a variety of shapes and colors
* Two sheets of wax paper large enough to accommodate your child's leaves (waxed sides must face each other, with the leaves sandwiched in-between.)
* Iron, set on low

INSTRUCTIONS:
Allow your child to have time to choose the leaves they want to preserve and then to arrange them on the wax paper. At this point, your supervision is highly recommended since you must iron the wax paper to seal it. Gently press the iron on the paper and hold to seal. You will probably see the wax melt together as you do this. Once the wax paper is cool enough to touch, you may display it as you wish.

FINAL THOUGHTS:
You can cut the wax paper sheets into a different shape for each design: Hexagons, circles, hearts, or whatever your child considers attractive.

Once again our often used window comes in handy here. When you suspend the waxed leaf design in front of a sunny window, it takes on a stained glass appearance, especially if you use leaves brilliant in fall colors.

In our family, we make this a full day project. We head off to a nature preserve in our area and hike the trails while collecting fallen leaves, acorns and pine cones. We bring along a folder to press the leaves in for the trip home, and then once home, we preserve our memory of a beautiful fall day!

If you are unable to get out to find colored leaves, a nice substitute for this project is to use crayon shavings. Using a butter knife, scrape/shave a few colored crayons and sprinkle the shavings onto the waxed paper. Be careful not to use too much, because the crayons, when they melt, have the tendency to ooze out the sides of the paper. Depending upon which colors you choose, you are able to make some interesting designs and patterns to create a real "stained glass" effect.

INTENSITY LEVEL: * * * (Three Stars)

Lesson 33
Drawing Bunnies

PURPOSE:
In this lesson, your child will be taught how to draw a rabbit using the five elements of shape.

MATERIALS NEEDED:
* Art Pattern #6 (page 69)
* Crayons, markers, colored pencils or other drawing tools
* Extra white paper

INSTRUCTIONS:
Using Art Pattern #6, have your child copy the development of the bunny on a separate piece of white paper. After drawing the head and body, the hind-legs, (generally the most difficult part), can be simplified by telling your child to draw a looping "3". Finally, add the front legs, tail and facial features.

It is easier if your child first draws the bunny in pencil, following the instructions, and then erases the unnecessary lines. After your child understands the shapes and concepts presented, he can try drawing the bunny in pen. Encourage your child to add to the picture by drawing grass, trees, buildings, water, other bunnies, etc.

Please feel free to photo copy Art Pattern #6 for additional practice with your child or other family members.

INTENSITY LEVEL: * * * (Three Stars)

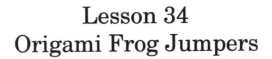

Lesson 34
Origami Frog Jumpers

PURPOSE:
In this lesson, your child will learn more about the art of origami. The frog, which they will make, can actually jump when pressure is applied to its lower back.

MATERIALS NEEDED:
* Art Pattern #21 (page 101)
* Scissors
* Colored pencils, crayons or markers

INSTRUCTIONS:
Cut out the origami design from the paper by trimming along the solid black line. The dimensions of the rectangle should be approximately 5 1/4 X 7 3/4 inches.

-- Mountain fold line 1, crease the line then unfold.
-- Mountain fold line 2, crease the line then unfold.
-- Valley fold line 3, crease the line then unfold. Your folds should now look like an "X" with a line through the middle.
-- Push together sections A and B so that the center of the "X", becomes a point. Section C should now be underneath the head of the frog.
-- Flip frog to back side and valley fold lines 4 and 5. Crease into position.
-- Valley fold lines 6 and 7 and crease into position.
-- Flip frog back to front and "S" fold lines 8 and 9. Line 8 will be a valley fold and line 9 will be a mountain fold. This section will act as the "spring" to propel the frog.

Gently press upon the "+" to send him leaping. Your child may color the frog after he has finished folding it.

Mountain Fold

Valley Fold

FINAL THOUGHTS:
The ancient art of origami is a fascinating study, which is limited only by one's own imagination. If your child enjoys creating interesting objects from paper, you may wish to go to your local library or bookstore and see what materials they have available on origami.

INTENSITY LEVEL: * * * (Three Stars)

Lesson 35
Grow Your Own Yard

PURPOSE:
This lesson will give your child the chance to watch seeds develop and then to care for their own little parcel of land.

MATERIALS NEEDED:
* Ten inch clay saucer or any growing receptacle you wish to use
* Dirt
* Plastic Wrap
* Quick growing rye or grass seed
* Newspapers to cover work area

INSTRUCTIONS:
Choose the dirt you wish to use for planting. This can be garden dirt which has been sifted, potting soil, or a mix of potting soil and vermiculite. Have your child fill a planting dish with the dirt, about 3/4 of the way full. Lightly sow the seeds across the soil and then sprinkle very lightly with dirt (about 1/16 of an inch). At this point, water extremely gently and cover the pot with plastic wrap stretched taut. As soon as the seeds sprout, remove the plastic to prevent molding.

Growth time depends upon the type of seed used, but generally after about 2-3 weeks you will have a yard of lush green grass which can be "mowed" with scissors.

Once the seeds sprout, lightly water the grass every couple of days, or whenever the soil needs it. Advise your child not to water the grass too much, lest the EPA come in and declare the potted yard a "wetland"!

FINAL THOUGHTS:
Tiny silk flowers can be placed amongst the blades of grass to look like wild flowers growing in the meadow.

Our family grew this potted yard one spring and added tiny ceramic rabbits to it. We invited friends over, and this became the centerpiece on the children's table at a brunch in our home. It was a real hit with everyone.

If for some reason you cannot obtain grass seeds, you may try purchasing a small packet of wild flower seeds to grow. The important thing here, is that the child have an opportunity to observe stages of growth in plant life and experience the beauty of God's creation.

INTENSITY LEVEL: * * (Two Stars)

Lesson 36
Paper Birdhouse

PURPOSE:
In this lesson, your child will be able to create an indoor birdhouse made of paper. This lesson can be used as an impetus toward the investigation of the many habitats of our feathered friends.

MATERIALS NEEDED:
* Art Pattern #22 (page 103)
* Scissors
* Glue or glue stick
* 3 X 4 inch piece of cardboard (from cereal box or other available source)
* Crayons, markers, colored pencils or other coloring tools

INSTRUCTIONS:
Using Art Pattern #22, have your child decorate the front, back and sides of the soon-to-be birdhouse. Next, cut the birdhouse pattern from the paper, following the solid lines. Also, cut out the circle to make an entrance to the birdhouse. Fold, as indicated by dotted lines and glue the tabs together to form the shape. It may be necessary for you to help your child with the folding and gluing in this project. Glue the bottom tab to your piece of cardboard to form a base. If your child wants to cut out and color the bird, he may then glue this to the top or front of the house.

FINAL THOUGHTS:
Bird watching is both a fun and educational hobby. Our family had a clear acrylic, window birdhouse for several years. It was so much fun to watch the cardinals come each day and then bring their babies in the spring and summer to feed. If you have a good window for observation, this kind of birdhouse could prove to be a great investment.

Birdhouses themselves have become a huge collectable lately. Both antique and newly crafted birdhouses are much sought after. Perhaps you and your child could investigate the wide range of functional and fanciful birdhouses available and share this hobby together.

INTENSITY LEVEL: * * * (Three Stars)

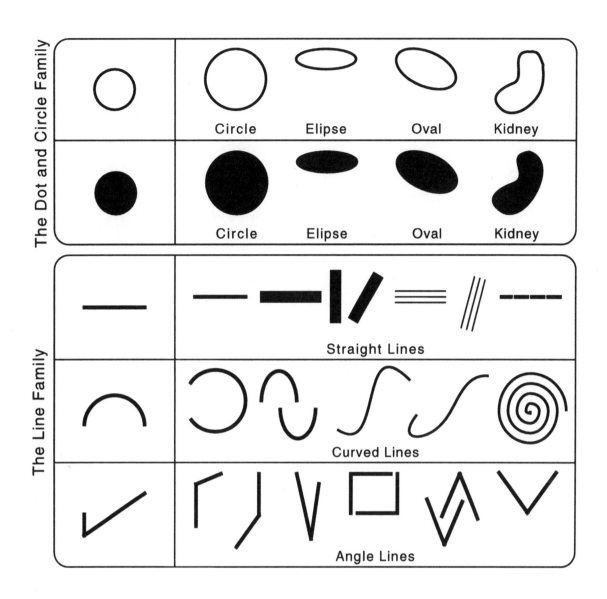

The Dot and Circle Family

Circle Elipse Oval Kidney

Circle Elipse Oval Kidney

The Line Family

Straight Lines

Curved Lines

Angle Lines

*Idea for the five elements of shape borrowed from
Drawing With Children by Mona Brookes

The Dot and Circle Family

	Circle Elipse Oval Kidney
○	Circle Elipse Oval Kidney
●	Circle Elipse Oval Kidney

The Line Family

―	Straight Lines
⌒	Curved Lines
✓	Angle Lines

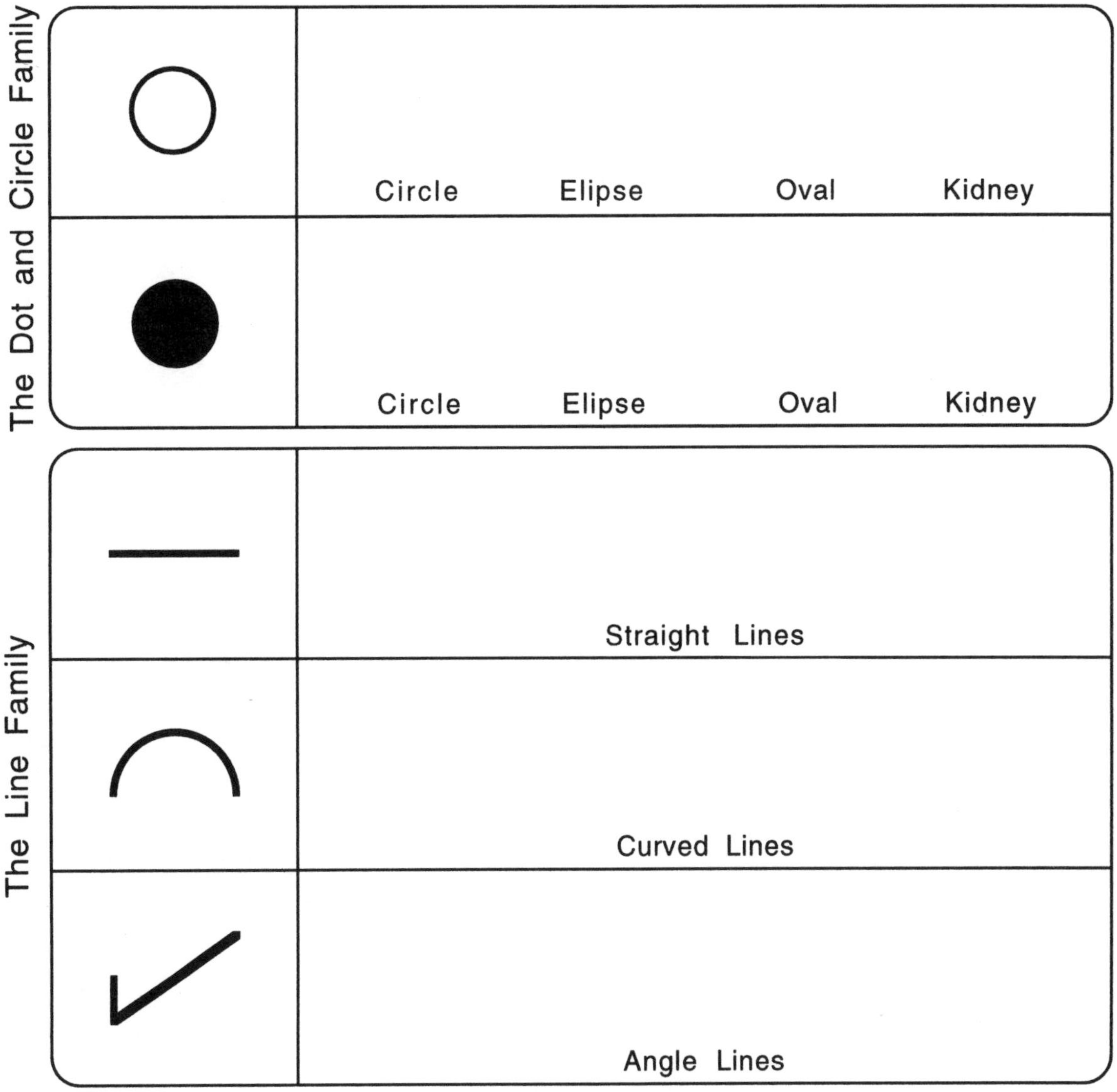

*Idea for the five elements of shape borrowed from
<u>Drawing With Children</u> by Mona Brookes

The Face of a Fox

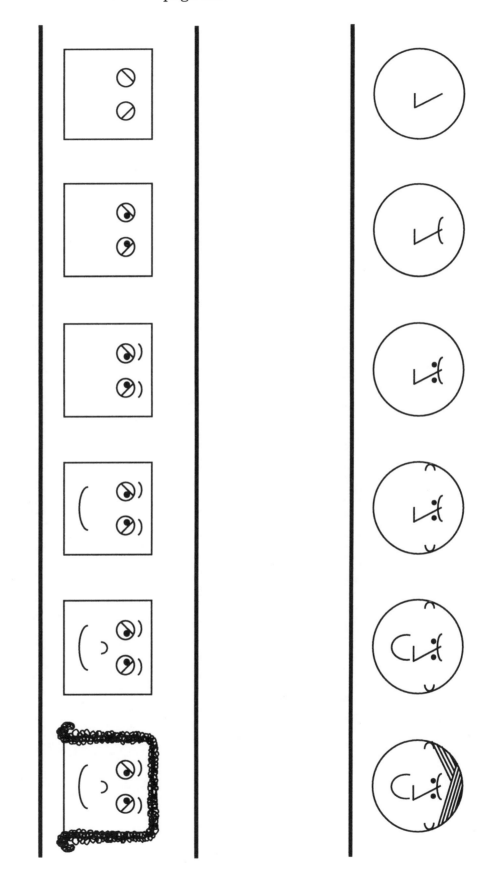

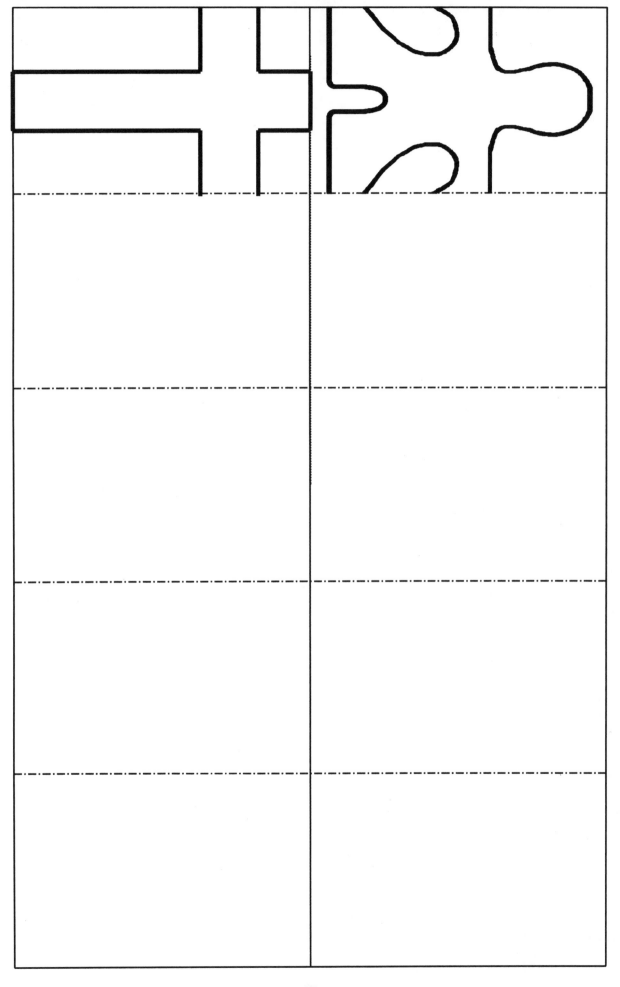

Art Pattern #6, to be used with Lesson #33, page 53.

Step 1   Step 2   Step 3

Step 4   Step 5

Art Pattern #9, to be used with Lesson #8,
page 13.

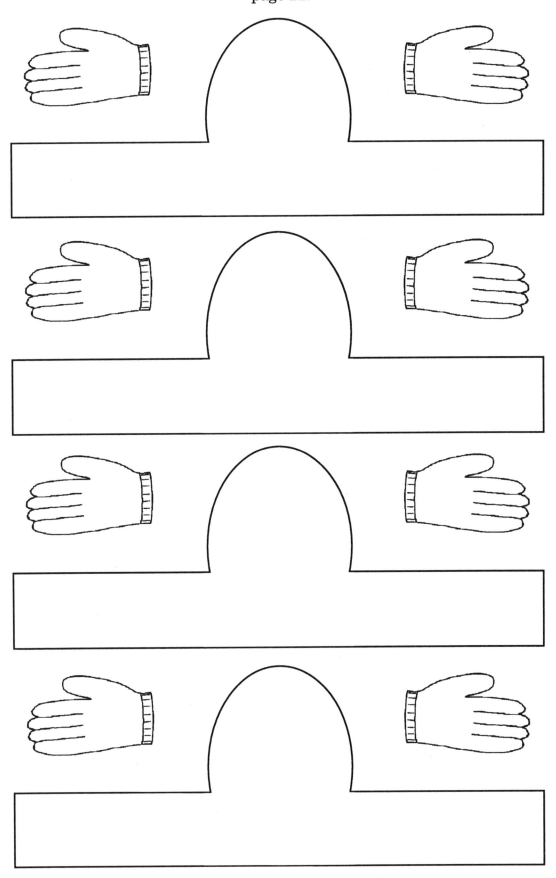

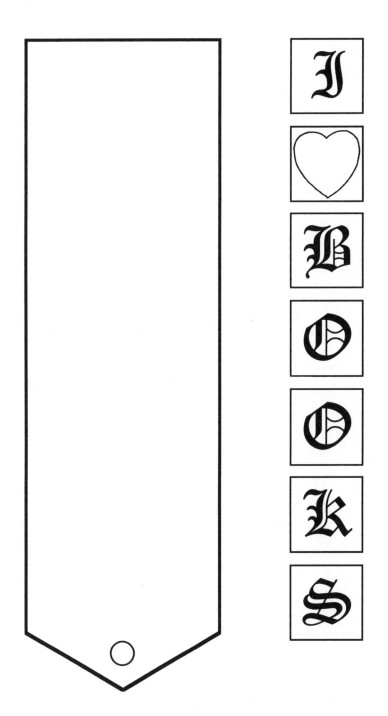

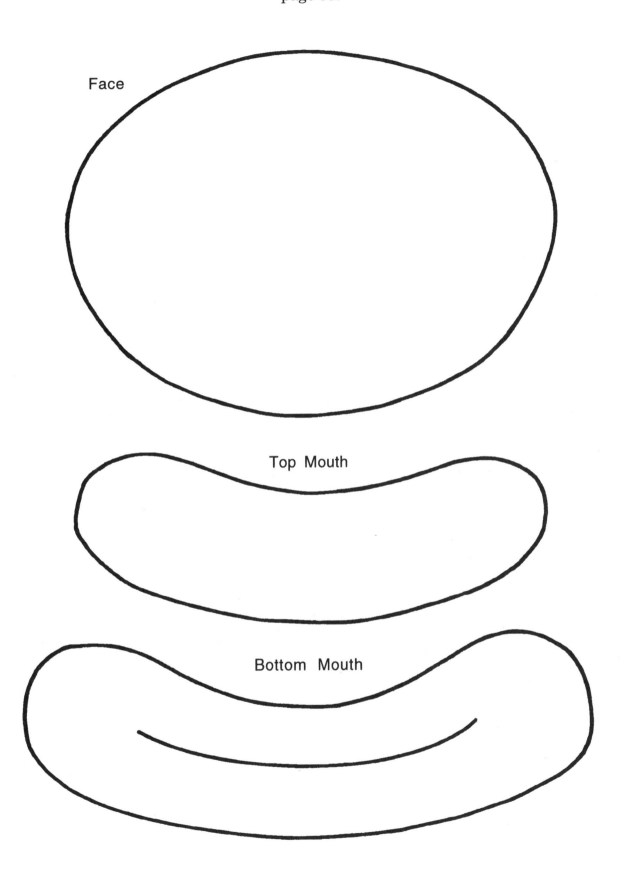

Face

Top Mouth

Bottom Mouth

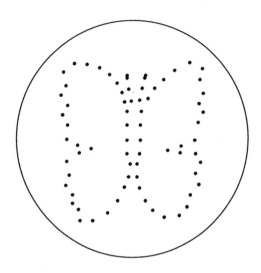

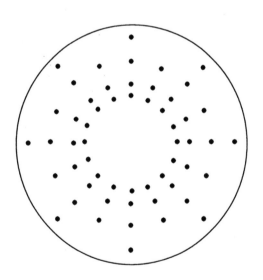

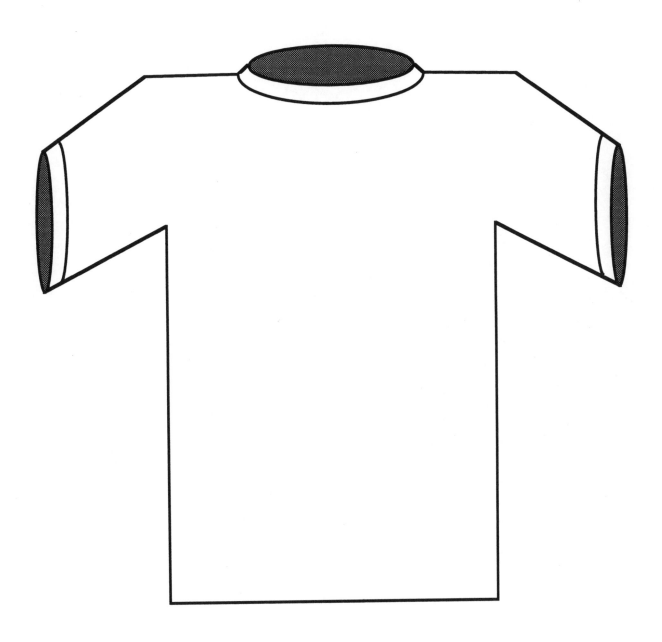

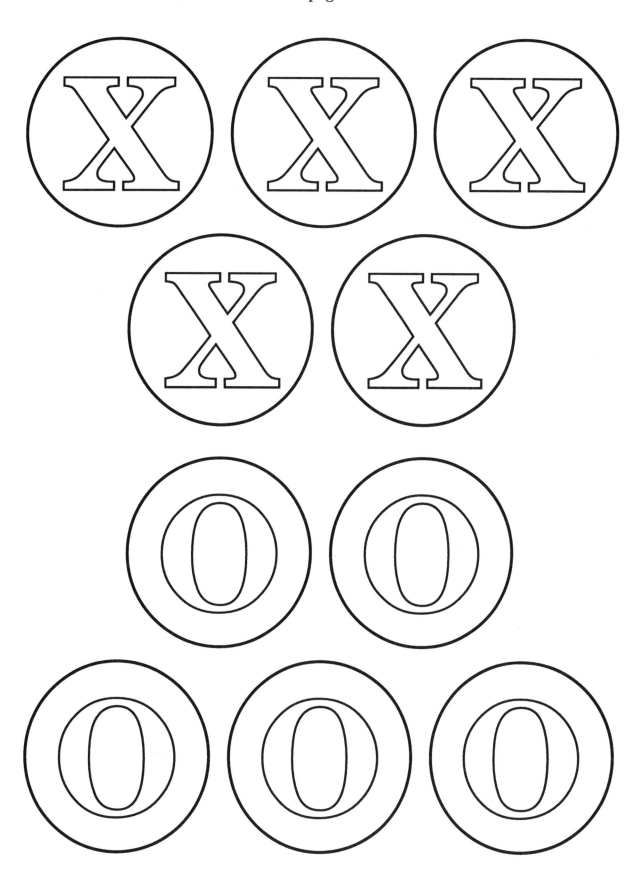

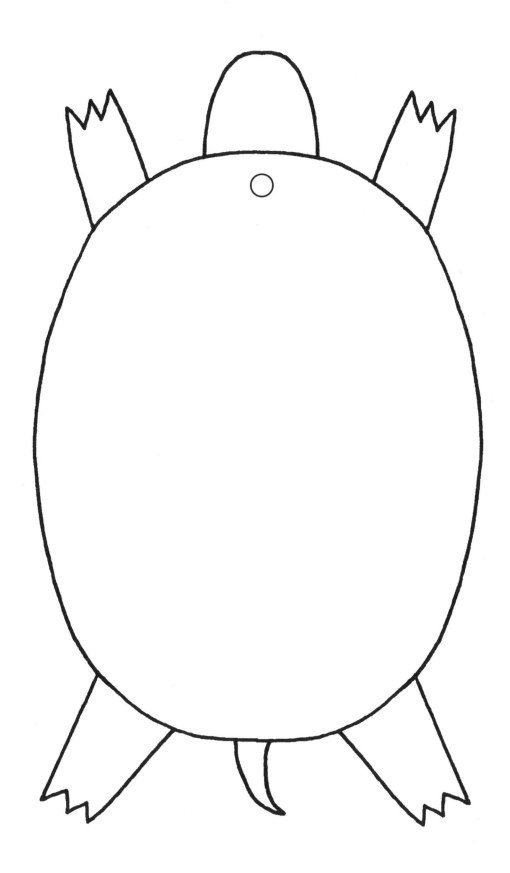

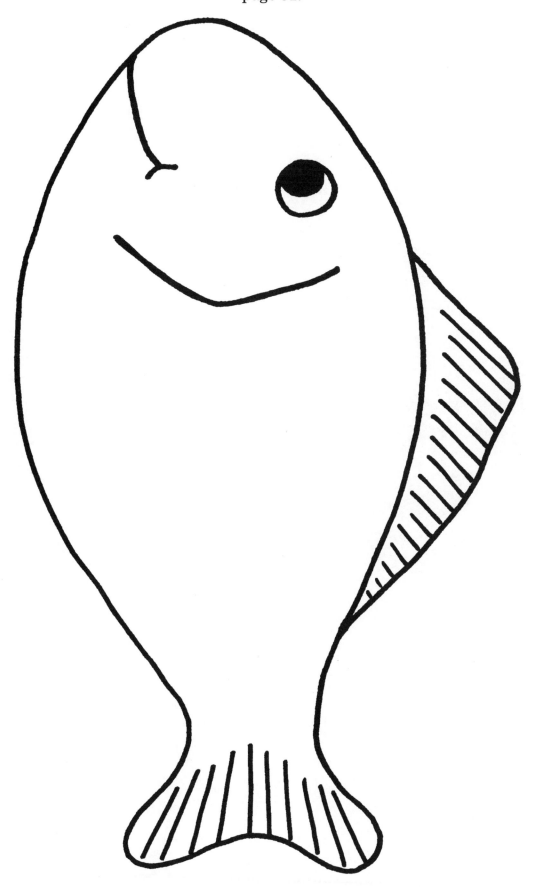

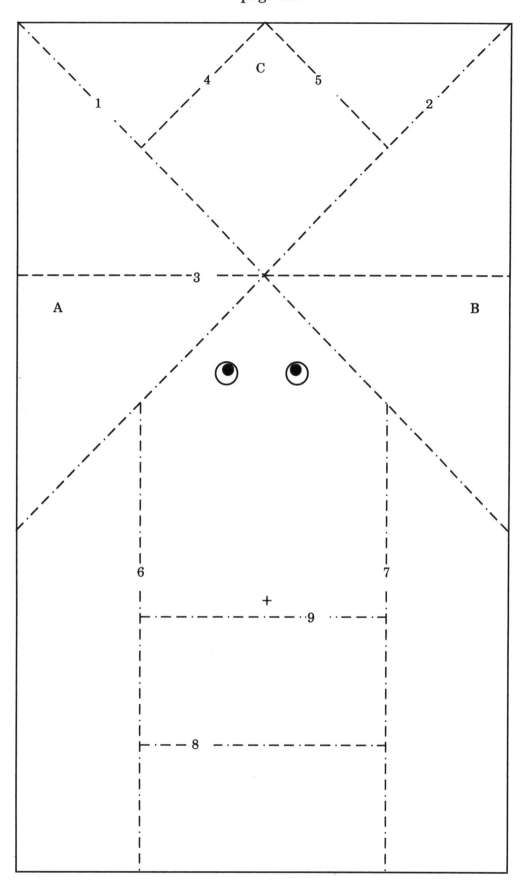

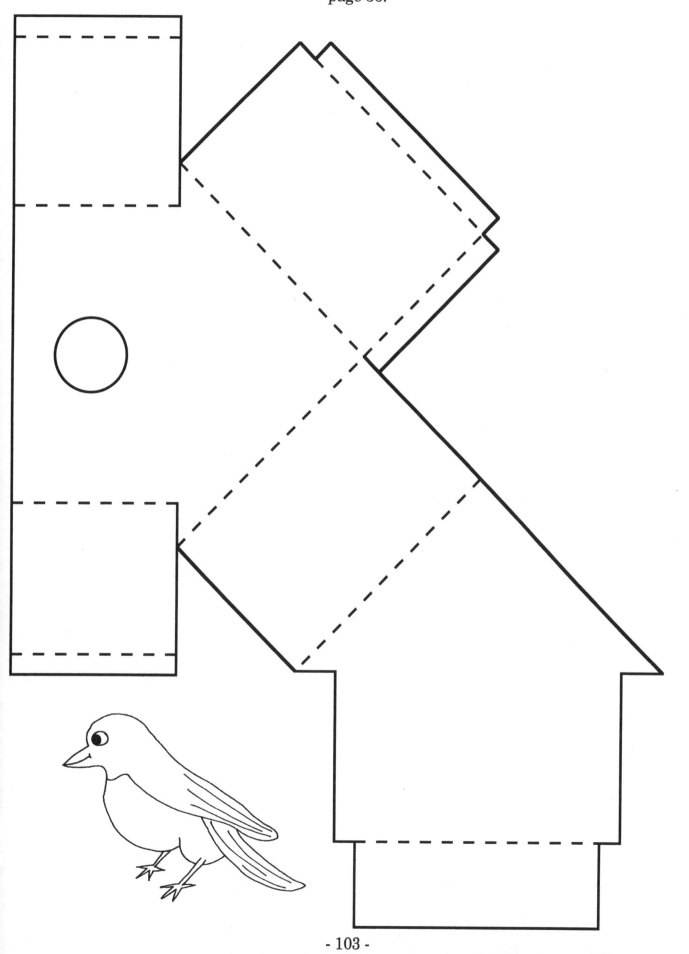

Art Pattern #22, to be used with Lesson #36, page 56.